To my students, who taught me more than I taught them

To my mother and husband, both of whom encouraged me to follow my dreams

To my daughter, whom I love

—K. L.

For Lucy, Nancy, and Rocky

—T. G.

References

I began my research with www.dumblaws.com but included only laws that were corroborated by a second source.
—K.L.

Bartlett, John, and Justin Kaplan. *Bartlett's Familiar Quotations.* Boston: Little, Brown and Company, 1992.

Compton's Interactive Encyclopedia Deluxe, 1997, s.v. "Magna Carta."

Documents from Old Testament Times, "The Hammurabi Steele." Partially retold in English by Stan Rummel, director of the humanities program at Texas Wesleyan University, Fort Worth, Texas.

Hyman, Dick. *The Columbus Chicken Statute and More Bonehead Legislation.* Lexington, Mass.: Stephen Greene Press, 1985.

———. *The Trenton Pickle Ordinance and Other Bonehead Legislation.* Brattleboro, Vt.: Stephen Greene Press, 1976.

Microsoft Encarta 98, 1993–97, s.v. "Susan B. Anthony," "Intolerable Acts," "Stamp Act."

Seuling, Barbara. *You Can't Eat Peanuts in Church and Other Little-Known Laws.* New York: Doubleday, 1975.

The World Almanac and Book of Facts, 2000, s.v. "U.S. Constitution."

Text copyright © 2002 by Kathi Linz
Illustrations copyright © 2002 by Tony Griego

All rights reserved. For information about permission to reproduce selections from this book, write to Permissions, Houghton Mifflin Company, 215 Park Avenue South, New York, New York 10003.

www.houghtonmifflinbooks.com

The text of this book is set in Stone Informal
The illustrations are pen and ink and watercolor.

Library of Congress Cataloging-in-Publication Data
Linz, Kathi.
Chickens may not cross the road and other crazy (but true) laws / by Kathi Linz ; illustrated by Tony Griego.
p. cm.
Includes bibliographical references.
Summary: A collection of humorous laws from across the country, along with information on why we have laws and how they are established.
ISBN 0-618-11257-X
1. Law—United States—Humor—Juvenile literature. [1. Law—Humor. 2. Law—History.] I. Griego, Tony, ill. II. Title.
K184.L569 2002   348.73'02—dc 21   2001051626

Printed in Hong Kong
SCP 10 9 8 7 6 5 4 3 2 1

WHY DO WE HAVE SUCH CRAZY LAWS?

All of the laws in this book either are or once were on the state law books. But how can our cities or states pass such crazy laws?

Some strange-sounding laws exist to keep people safe. In California, it's illegal to lick toads (even if you wanted to). Why? One kind of toad oozes poison through its skin. Some people got a druglike high by licking it. The law was written to keep people from harming themselves with toad poison.

But there are hundreds and hundreds of laws that just plain don't make sense. In Texas, "If two trains meet each other on the same track, they must both stop and wait until the other one has passed." (Huh? That means neither train can move.) Or, in Belvedere, California, "No dog can appear in public without its master on a leash." (Someone should have paid attention to the language teacher.) And we can only guess why any government would pass a law about keeping *elephants* on leashes.

It is illegal
To Tie a
Crocodile
To a Fire Hydrant.
(michigan State Law)

How About Having NO LAWS?

Since such stupid laws get passed, how about having no rules? What fun! But what if no one stopped at a stop sign? What if the neighborhood bully was allowed to steal your bike? Or if it were fine for someone to shoot your dog or cat? What if someone really *did* tie a crocodile to the fire hydrant in front of your house? Okay, so that probably won't happen, but wise laws—like those against stealing, murder, and arson—help people live together peacefully.

"Law is order, and good law is good order."
—Socrates, ancient Greek philosopher

"Laws should be like clothes.
They should fit the people they serve."
—Clarence Darrow, U.S. lawyer

"Law is order, and good law is good order."

WHAT IS THE OLDEST SET OF LAWS EVER WRITTEN?

Almost 3,000 years ago, a man named Hammurabi became king of Babylon (where Iraq is today). His law code was used for more than 500 years. Some of his laws don't sound very fair to us today...

If a free person puts out another free person's eye, that person's eye shall be put out.

If a son strikes his father, his hand shall be cut off.

If a slave strikes the cheek of a free person, the slave's ear shall be cut off.

ONLY the FIRST FOUR FIREMEN To ARRive at a Fire Will Be Paid. (Zeigler, ILLinois)

You may not swim on dry land.

(Santa Ana, California)

WE, the PEOPLE oF the UNITED STATES, HAVE Rights, RiGHT?

"We were the first people in history to found a nation . . . governed by 'We the People.'" —Warren E. Burger, Chief Justice of the United States

What laws would *you* like to see get passed? If you think something is important enough to require a law, you can write to elected people in your area and tell them your ideas. Write your idea, or petition, on a sheet of paper. Have many people sign the bottom of the sheet to show that they agree with you. Then send it to elected officials.

Once the officials agree that your idea is important, they write it up as a bill and present it to the state or national assembly for a vote. If more officials vote for it than against it, the governor or president signs it. Then it becomes a law.

Here is a good example of people working to pass a new law: In 1851, Susan B. Anthony decided that women deserved to vote. At that time, only men were allowed the privilege of voting. She held meetings, published a newspaper, and wrote to important people about granting women the right to vote. As part of her protest, Susan B. Anthony actually voted in the 1872 presidential election. (She was arrested and fined $100!)

For women to vote, the Constitution had to be amended, which is difficult: two-thirds of the representatives and senators have to agree, then three-quarters of the states must agree. It took sixty-nine years of hard work but finally in 1920 the nineteenth amendment passed, giving women the right to vote.

If ANYONE is caught STEALING SOAP, He must wash himself WITH it UNTIL He uses it UP. (MoVAVE COUNTY, ARIZONA)

Legislative Branch—A group of elected people who decide which ideas (bills) should become laws.

In the United States we have two "houses" that vote on bills—the *House of Representatives* and the *Senate.* More than half of each house has to vote in favor of the bill before it is sent to . . .

The Executive Branch—Which includes the president (at the state level it is the governor), the vice president (lieutenant governor at state level), and the president's closest advisors, who are called the Cabinet.

The president may talk to any of the advisors before deciding if the bill should become a law. The president either signs the bill, making it a law, or vetoes it, stopping it from becoming a law. Once a bill is signed, the only thing that can stand in the way is . . .

The UNITED States

The Judicial Branch—Headed by the Supreme Court.
Whenever necessary the justices on the Supreme Court look at a new law and compare it with the Constitution of the United States. If they think the new law goes against the Constitution, they can say it is "unconstitutional." Then it will no longer be a law.

The writers of the Constitution made sure no one person could make all the rules. This system is called "checks and balances." The president can sign only laws that have been passed by the House of Representatives and the Senate. If the Supreme Court thinks something is unconstitutional, it won't be a law no matter *who* voted for it!

The Power of the People
But no one can vote for any law at all unless the people choose him or her to be part of their government. The people have the power to elect legislators; to tell them what is important to their town, state, or country; and to vote them out of office when they disagree with them. The people can also go to legislators and tell them when they think a law is dumb. Any law can be repealed, or withdrawn.

"No man is good enough to govern another man without that man's consent."
—Abraham Lincoln, Sixteenth U.S. President

AUTHOR'S NOTE

Many laws are just plain crazy no matter how you word them, but some sound less crazy in their original form. For example, the California Fish and Game Code has a three-page list of animals that may not be kept as pets. It's funnier to pick out the oddest animal in the list: "It is illegal to keep slugs or land snails as pets."

Many of the laws in this book were established during the end of the 1800s and the early part of the 1900s. Our country changed quickly in the twentieth century, going from hand and horse labor to machines; we learned how to drive cars, fly planes, and dry our clothes in a machine. That rapid change gave us laws like "Drivers of motor vehicles must come to a stop if they scare a horse" and "It is against the law to drive a car into town without calling City Hall first."

Some of these laws went out of date and were repealed. The rest are still on the books but are not enforced because they don't work with our new ways of doing things. And, well, they aren't enforced because they just don't make any sense.

The UNITED States

The Judicial Branch—Headed by the Supreme Court.
Whenever necessary the justices on the Supreme Court look at a new law and compare it with the Constitution of the United States. If they think the new law goes against the Constitution, they can say it is "unconstitutional." Then it will no longer be a law.

The writers of the Constitution made sure no one person could make all the rules. This system is called "checks and balances." The president can sign only laws that have been passed by the House of Representatives and the Senate. If the Supreme Court thinks something is unconstitutional, it won't be a law no matter *who* voted for it!

The Power of the People
But no one can vote for any law at all unless the people choose him or her to be part of their government. The people have the power to elect legislators; to tell them what is important to their town, state, or country; and to vote them out of office when they disagree with them. The people can also go to legislators and tell them when they think a law is dumb. Any law can be repealed, or withdrawn.

"No man is good enough to govern another man without that man's consent."
—Abraham Lincoln, Sixteenth U.S. President

Author's Note

Many laws are just plain crazy no matter how you word them, but some sound less crazy in their original form. For example, the California Fish and Game Code has a three-page list of animals that may not be kept as pets. It's funnier to pick out the oddest animal in the list: "It is illegal to keep slugs or land snails as pets."

Many of the laws in this book were established during the end of the 1800s and the early part of the 1900s. Our country changed quickly in the twentieth century, going from hand and horse labor to machines; we learned how to drive cars, fly planes, and dry our clothes in a machine. That rapid change gave us laws like "Drivers of motor vehicles must come to a stop if they scare a horse" and "It is against the law to drive a car into town without calling City Hall first."

Some of these laws went out of date and were repealed. The rest are still on the books but are not enforced because they don't work with our new ways of doing things. And, well, they aren't enforced because they just don't make any sense.